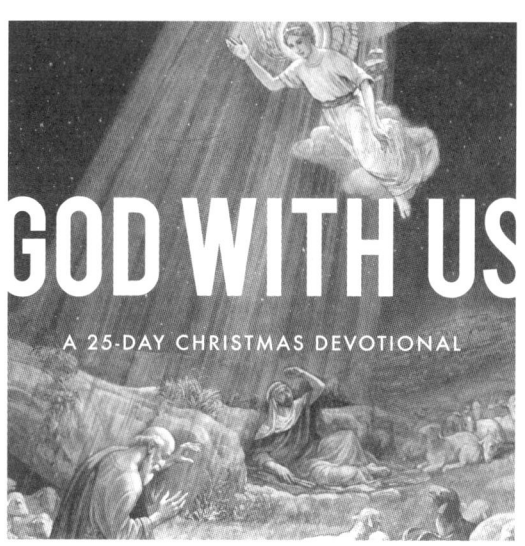

GOD WITH US

A 25-DAY CHRISTMAS DEVOTIONAL

BY ANDY BLANKS

PUBLISHED BY YM360

INTRODUCTION

What is something extraordinary that you take for granted?

How about your phone? We rarely think about how incredible the technology is you have in your hand. Just a few years before you were born, the kind of technology you walk around with every day would have been unthinkable.

What about the human body? You don't think about it, but consider how incredibly complicated a simple act, such as reaching for the remote control, is. You somehow decide to reach for it, and your brain fires all these signals to your nerves, which move your muscles to reach out and grasp something a few feet away from you. It's stunning how miraculous this simple action is.

Why don't we think about how cool these seemingly random things are? Because they are so routine. We do them so often we don't think about them. We lose the wonder because of how seemingly normal it is.

The same is true when it comes to how we think about Christmas. And we HAVE to change this.

Christmas can be a time when we get so wrapped up in the commercial (and chaotic) aspects of the season that we lose sight of the spiritual aspect. We are so familiar with the story that we can forget how amazing it is. God, the eternal, unchanging God who spoke the universe into being, came to our earth in the form of a fragile, human baby. And He did this to save us from the penalty of our sins so that we could be in relationship with Him. THAT is the most amazing story ever told. And we need to do whatever we can to keep from losing our awe of this story.

That's what this book helps you do. Each day, from December 1 to Christmas morning, you will be walking through the Christmas story, the moment when God became human. You'll be challenged to be moved by this story and to see your life and faith differently. There are even family devotionals for Christmas Eve and Christmas Day.

Prepare your heart and mind to celebrate the most wonderful story ever told.

DAY

DEVOTIONAL PASSAGE: LUKE 1:5-7

Waiting is something most people struggle with (even though these days, waiting in line or for someone to show up at a restaurant means you get extra time to check social media or play a video game on your phone). We're impatient by nature. But the funny thing is that God often sees waiting in a different light than we do. God will sometimes make us wait so that we learn to appreciate what He has already planned to reveal to us.

Read Luke 1:5-7. What do we learn about Zechariah and Elizabeth here? We learn Zechariah is a priest. We learn Elizabeth is the daughter of priestly heritage (that's what the whole "daughters of Aaron" means). We learn that they are righteous. But we also learn something about them in verse 7: they have been waiting for a child that has not come.

The theme of "waiting" runs through the Christmas narrative, but it's easy for us to miss it if we don't know the backstory. If we go back to the time of David, something like 1,000 years before Jesus was born, God was continually speaking through His prophets. If you were an Israelite during those days, God's presence seemed like a constant thing. But as the Israelites were repeatedly unfaithful to God, He chose to speak predictions of judgment through His prophets, warning the people what would happen if they didn't turn back to God. With each message of judgment, there was also the promise of future hope when the Messiah would come. But the people never listened to the message. Judgment came as God promised it would. The people were scattered and defeated.

Then, as far as we know, God went silent. For close to 400 years, we have no recorded revelation from God. God was not absent, but He was quiet. God was letting His people wait. They had been waiting in anticipation for the Messiah to come. They had been waiting for God to speak. They had been waiting for hundreds of years. But suddenly, this changed. The Christmas story is essentially about God breaking His silence and speaking into the void. The wait was over. God was moving, and nothing would ever be the same.

THINK ABOUT THIS:

• Why is waiting on God difficult at times?
• What can you do to keep your faith strong as you wait?

DEVOTIONAL PASSAGE: LUKE 1:8-23

Surprises. Sometimes surprises are good. And sometimes surprises are not so good. When your parents tell you you're going to the beach after Christmas? Good surprise. When your coach informs you that today's practice will be nothing but conditioning? Bad surprise. New phone for your birthday? Good surprise. Pop-quiz? Bad surprise.

A surprise is nothing more than being caught unprepared. If your parents said to you, "Just a head's up. Tomorrow we're going to tell you that we're going on a super-fun vacation," when it came time for the announcement, you wouldn't be surprised. You would have been prepared for it. God likes surprises as much as the next person. Isn't the heart of every miracle a surprise? But God also understands the value of preparation. And in today's passage, we see how preparation is woven into the Christmas narrative.

Read Luke 1:8-23, paying special attention to verses 16 and 17. You were introduced to Zechariah yesterday. In this passage, we see Zechariah going about his priestly duties when God chose to surprise him. Zechariah met an angel who had an important announcement: Zechariah and Elizabeth would be the parents of a special child. Not just any child, but John the Baptist. What an epic announcement.

Look closely at verses 16-17. This is a prophecy about the nature of John the Baptist's life's work. John would give his life to preparing people for the coming Messiah. In God's great plan to send Jesus to earth to live among His people, He wanted John there, calling people to prepare themselves to encounter Jesus. I believe there is a powerful truth for us here, as well.

As we navigate the Christmas season in our 21st Century culture, it's easy to forget what we're building toward. Ideally, each day that draws closer to December 25 is another day we're preparing to encounter Jesus. Not literally, as the people in John's world would do. But preparing our hearts and minds to celebrate the amazing, world-changing story of Jesus' birth. If we don't intentionally prepare ourselves, the real risk is that Christmas passes us by, and we've not been moved by it.

God knew that preparation was important for people in the 1st Century. It's no less important for us today.

THINK ABOUT THIS:

- What do you need to do to prepare yourself for a meaningful Christmas season?
- Is there anything in your life that is an obstacle to your preparation? What would it take for you to remove that obstacle for this Christmas season?

DEVOTIONAL PASSAGE: LUKE 1:24-25

Have you ever been accused of something you didn't do? It could have been something small or something big. No matter what it is, when you get blamed for something, it's a terrible feeling, especially when you know that you didn't do anything wrong.

Read Luke 1:24-25. We're continuing with the story of Zechariah and Elizabeth. They are an important (if sometimes forgotten) part of the Christmas story. We can learn from them a great deal, but we may have to look a little more closely to find it. In today's passage, it's easy to skip over the really powerful truth contained within it. So let's take a moment to slow down a bit.

Why did Elizabeth hide for so long? To understand this, we have to understand what the word "reproach" means. In verse 25, Elizabeth says the Lord "looked on [her], to take away [her] reproach among people." The word reproach means "an expression of disapproval or disappointment." What was going on? What had Elizabeth done wrong that people would disapprove of? In a word, nothing. But that didn't keep people from treating her as if she had.

In Elizabeth's culture, when a woman was unable to have a child, it was seen as a sign of God's judgment. People assumed that if a woman couldn't have a child, she must be living in such a way that God was displeased with her. Now, certainly, Elizabeth wasn't perfect. But the Bible describes her and Zechariah as "righteous." Nowadays, we know that the inability to have a baby is due to biological reasons. But Elizabeth had lived her life under the judgment of others. In a sense, she had been accused of something she didn't do. So not only was she happy that God would be giving her a son, but she had to be incredibly, amazingly relieved that God was clearing her name, freeing her from the undeserved judgment of others.

Freedom. Freedom from judgment. Freedom from guilt. Freedom from sin. Jesus' birth over 2,000 years ago signified all of these things. Not just for Elizabeth, but for all people everywhere who would come to believe in Jesus.

THINK ABOUT THIS:

• What are some words that describe how Elizabeth must have felt when God took away her reproach?
• Have you ever thought about how it makes you feel when you consider the fact that Jesus has done the same for you? Express to God how it makes you feel when you think about Him removing your sin, guilt, and shame.

DEVOTIONAL PASSAGE: LUKE 1:26-33

If your family has ever received a birth announcement in the mail, you know that they're pretty cool. You've seen these, right? Baby is born. Mom and dad dress baby up in a super-cute outfit (or go the minimalist route and show the baby in his/her birthday suit). The picture is taken and, most likely, uploaded to a site that specializes in birth announcements. And then, all the details are added. Full name. Date of birth. Weight and length at the time of birth. And maybe even a statement from mom and dad: "Our family is pleased to announce the birth of . . ." Some are elaborate. Some are simple. But all are intended to let the world know the existence of a treasured new arrival.

Read Luke 1:26-33. This was a birth announcement unlike any other in history. No uploaded pics to a website. No US Postal service involved. This was a DM straight from God to Mary. Can you imagine? Mary is minding her business when an actual angel just appears. We can understand why she would be afraid! And look at what the angel said to Mary. This is the heart of this most amazing birth announcement.

The language the angel used to announce to Mary of the news of her pending pregnancy would have rocked Mary's world. "Son of the Most High." "Throne of his father, David." "Reign over the house of Jacob." "No end to his kingdom." This language, these words, would have signified to Mary that this baby was the long-awaited Messiah. The messenger and the message told her that she was about to be a part of something bigger than anything she could have imagined. Everything about her life and the world was about to change.

There is no way we can even begin to process what Mary must have been feeling. The angel's announcement signified that God was working His plan to bridge the gap in history. The birth of Jesus signified the connecting of the narrative thread from the Old Testament to the New. God was continuing His faithfulness to His people but in a new, bigger way. The nature of the game was changing. Jesus was God with us. Emmanuel! This was a birth announcement unlike any other. And it changed the course of history.

THINK ABOUT THIS:

• The announcement that Jesus would be born was a game-changer. How has God been a game-changer in your life? Think of three ways your life is different because you know and are known by Jesus.

DAY

DEVOTIONAL PASSAGE: LUKE 1:34-38

I don't understand. That doesn't make sense. How is that possible?

Each of these phrases expresses a similar emotion: confusion. Maybe you can remember the last time you were really confused about something. Maybe it's been a while. But we've all been there. Faced with a situation we can't quite figure out, we just sort of shake our head, confused about the outcome.

Read Luke 1:34-38. Here, Mary is confused. And rightly so. The angel has just told her she was going to have a baby. Mary, confused, wonders how in the world this is going to happen, considering she is not married and has never been with a man. The angel's reply is powerful in its simplicity: "Don't worry. God's going to take care of it." Huh?

Do you wonder if Mary had a ton of questions? The Holy Spirit is going to be the dad? Will I know when it happens? Will the baby need nine months to grow like normal? Or will he just appear one day? What will people say? Are you sure you've got the right girl? Maybe she had a lot of questions. We don't know. What we know is that Mary responded to the amazing news with one phrase. Looking at this messenger of God standing in her living room, she simply said, "I'm the Lord's servant. If you say so, I'm on board."

Mary's faith is remarkable. She instantly trusted God, even though she could not have had any idea of how God's plan would work out. She didn't know HOW it would work, but she knew WHO was doing the work. And that made all the difference in the world.

The next time God leads you to do something you may not fully understand, remember Mary. Follow God's leading with the confidence that His plans are perfect.

THINK ABOUT THIS:
- Can you recall a time in your life when God led you to do something, and you didn't exactly know how it would turn out? What helped you to go through with it?
- What obstacles are standing in the way from you trusting God more? What do you need to do to remove these obstacles?

DAY   6

DEVOTIONAL PASSAGE: MATTHEW 1:18-19

Tension is an important aspect of great stories. Think about the last suspenseful movie you saw. There were most likely moments of tension throughout the movie. It's the moment when the hero is being chased. Will he get away? Or maybe the hero is trying to download secret documents from the bad guy's computer, and we know the bad guy is just about to walk in the room! Tension. It creates suspense. It creates a sense of expectation. It makes us cringe with excitement.

Sometimes, though, tension can be a bad thing, especially when it comes to relationships. Take a moment and read Matthew 1:18-19. Today's passage stops at verse 19 for a reason. It's a cliffhanger in the story. A moment of great tension. What will Joseph do? But it's more than this. Consider for a moment that Joseph isn't some make-believe character. He was a real man. A good man. And suddenly, his relationship was full of tension.

There are three moments we need to focus on. The moment Joseph decides to divorce Mary. The moment the angel comes to him and encourages him NOT to divorce Mary (we'll look at that moment tomorrow). And the moment he decides to heed the angel's advice and move forward with the engagement. We need to focus on the first two moments. How much time passed between the first and second moments? How long did God allow Joseph to live in the painful, heartbroken tension of feeling like his true love had been unfaithful to him?

Tension. Like many uncomfortable realities, God uses tension to teach us. When God allows you to walk through a season of tension, His desire is that it would turn your heart to Him, compelling you to seek Him in prayer. After all, Joseph's story worked out pretty well, didn't it? We have to trust that God is always working for His glory and our good. And we have to accept that He knows best.

Joseph's story is one full of tension and peace. But to find peace, we sometimes have to walk with God through moments of tension.

THINK ABOUT THIS:
- What other moments of tension can you recall in the Christmas story?
- If you can learn to see moments of tension in your life as God providing you a chance to seek Him more passionately, how do you think this might change your relationship with God?

DAY 7

DEVOTIONAL PASSAGE: MATTHEW 1:20-23

What are you scared of? Heights? Public speaking? Getting struck by lightning? Are you scared of snakes? Small spaces? Sharks? (If so, good. Sharks are insane, people-eating monsters. I mean, it's true.) Different folks are scared of different things. (Heck, you may even have chiraptophobia, the fear of being touched.) But there is one fear that most people struggle with, even if they never admit it—the fear of what other people will think.

You've probably felt this fear. It shows itself in funny ways sometimes. Like when you show up to school dressed for Tacky Day only to realize you have your dates off. Your big fear in a moment like this is that other people will laugh at you. But sometimes it's more serious than this. Sometimes, concerned about what others will say or do, we bury our true selves. We hide our faith. Or we try to be someone we're not. Fear of what people will think affects more of our decisions than we probably want to admit.

Read Matthew 1:20-23. We talked yesterday about the tension in Joseph's decision. The angel was about to cut right into this tension. But look at the first thing the angel says: "Do not fear to take Mary as your wife." The angel assures Joseph that Mary is telling the truth. But the first thing the angel said to Joseph had to do with what other people would think of him. Do not fear. This will be hard. You'll most likely get made fun of. People may even get upset with you and Mary. But don't worry about them. God is in control.

Christmas represents a perfect time to be bold about your faith. As our culture seeks to make Christmas about anything other than the birth of Jesus, it's a great chance for you to put the spotlight back on the true reason for the season. And so be encouraged by Joseph's example. Live your life without fear of what other people will think of you. Listen to God. Follow His ways. And live boldly for Him.

THINK ABOUT THIS:

- Why is it hard to be bold in our faith sometimes? What factors keep us from moving past what others think of us?
- What does your boldness, or lack thereof, say about your faith in God?

DAY 8

DEVOTIONAL PASSAGE: MATTHEW 1:24-25

Obedience is an interesting concept. It gets a bum rap. Just saying the word — "obedience" — kind of makes you shiver, doesn't it? Thinking about obeying brings to mind your mom telling you to take out the trash or clean your room. It recalls images of life in the slow lane, holding up traffic, driving the exact speed limit. There's a part of us ⊠ part cultural, part spiritual ⊠ that rebels at the notion of obeying the rules. (Think of this the next time you sneak candy into a movie theatre.)

And yet, obedience is firmly entrenched as a central part of what it means to be a Christ-follower. Jesus said in John 14, "Whoever has my commandments and keeps them, he it is who loves me . . . Whoever does not love me does not keep my words." That's pretty straightforward, isn't it?

So what does all this talk about obedience have to do with the Christmas story? Plenty. Read Matthew 1:24-25. We're wrapping up our three-day focus on Joseph's role in Jesus' birth story. This is the third snapshot we've studied. Joseph had decided to divorce Mary because of her pregnancy. Then, the angel encourages him not to do so, telling Joseph that the baby really is God's Son. But before we move on, let's pause here for a moment.

It's easy to breeze past "moments" in Scripture. Time is condensed. We don't always get a ton of details about what a person is feeling. If we're not careful, it's easy to act is if Joseph were a robot, not a real human being. But at that moment, when the angel had wrapped up his speech to Joseph, Joseph had a choice. A real choice. He could either obey God's will that he should marry Mary or he could disobey. We should recognize this choice, as it's one we make every day.

Joseph, the human being, made an amazing choice. He demonstrated his love for God by obeying: "When Joseph woke from sleep, he did as the angel of the Lord commanded him." Think of all that Joseph got to experience because he obeyed God! Think of how rich his life was as a result. If we believe in God, we must believe that what He has for us is awesome. Disobedience robs us from experiencing a full relationship with God. Joseph somehow understood this. And his faithfulness allowed him to be an awesome part of the greatest story ever told.

THINK ABOUT THIS:
• In your own words, what can we learn from Joseph's example?
• Our obedience is motivated by our love for God. Grab a piece of paper, or a note-taking app, and write down three reasons why you love God. Then thank Him in prayer for loving you.

DAY 9

DEVOTIONAL PASSAGE: LUKE 1:39-45

There's a feeling among people who don't believe in God that Christianity is a "no fun club." They look at Christianity as nothing but a bunch of rules to follow. Maybe you know people like this. They don't know God. And what keeps them from being open to it is a fear that God is nothing but a big wet blanket. The only issue with this is that joy is a huge part of what it means to be a Christ-follower.

The Bible is bursting with examples of happiness and joy flowing from God, and flowing from within those who follow Him. One of these examples is found in the awesome exchange between Mary and her cousin Elizabeth. Read Luke 1:39-45 as we pick up with these two women we were introduced to a few days ago.

Mary somehow caught wind of her cousin Elizabeth's news. Maybe the Lord gave Mary some insight to the other miraculous pregnancy in the works. Maybe Mary heard it through the family tree that Elizabeth was expecting in her old age. Whatever the case, Mary made a trip to see Elizabeth. What happens upon their seeing one another is an epic reunion. The two women greet each other with re-markable emotion. But the source of the emotion is where you'll focus your attention today.

Verse 42 shows us Elizabeth's reaction upon seeing Mary. Elizabeth "exclaims" with a "loud cry" that she is super-pumped to see her cousin. But look back to verse 41 at the source of this joy and celebration. The Holy Spirit filled Elizabeth! He was the source of her excitement. God empowered the happiness Elizabeth felt.

If we're not careful, we can view God in the same way that outsiders sometimes do. And yet God is the creator of all of our emotions. Happiness, joy, excitement, surprise, laughter . . . all of these originate with God. God takes joy in our joy. And if you take one thing from this book, let it be that your heart is to be JOYFUL this Christmas season. There is much to celebrate! Open your eyes. Take-in the moment. And allow the Holy Spirit to give birth to the joy within you at the birth of the King.

THINK ABOUT THIS:

• What about the Christmas season brings you joy? What makes you smile?
• Is there a particular Christmas song that makes you happy? Take the time to listen to it today (or if you're brave, sing it right now), and thank God for giving us the ability to experience joy and happiness.

DEVOTIONAL PASSAGE: LUKE 1:46-56

One of the things about our faith that makes it so unique is that it is intimately personal and universally general. Huh? Seriously, though. It's true. As individuals, we have this amazingly personal relationship with God. He knows us. He works in our lives for our good. We are His children. That's super personal. But at the same time, God's plan is HUUUUUUGE!!!!! He doesn't only work for us and within us. He works for and within all people. And all space. And all time. See? Personal and general.

Read Luke 1:46-56. Yesterday we looked at Elizabeth's powerful reaction of joy and happiness at the work God was doing. Today we'll look at Mary's response. But we're going to take a slightly different angle. We're not going to look at the part of her response that is personal to her, but at the part that is general to all people. Because nestled within Mary's prayer of praise to God for what He had done in her is a powerful declaration for what God has done for all people.

Re-read verses 52-55. Here we see one of the Christmas narrative's powerful truths: Jesus came to completely overturn our reality. The world says that the true rulers are those with power. Jesus came to show us that true power is found in humility. Jesus' life and teachings showed us that His people would be identified by service, not by pride. Over and over again, Jesus lifted the poor and oppressed and spoke convicting truth to those in power. Jesus demonstrated time after time that the spiritually needy will always find their fill if they honestly search for God. This is the heart of Mary's words here! It is as if she were predicting the ministry of Jesus, which, in a way, she was.

God's Kingdom is not like our world. God's ways are not like our ways. Jesus came to save the spiritually poor. He came to flip the order. The weak will be strong. The last will be first. He disturbed the status quo. As His children, our lives are meant to be lived in very much the same way.

THINK ABOUT THIS:

• As you go throughout the Christmas season, make sure that you're looking for opportunities to advance God's Kingdom on this earth. How are you lifting the weak? How are you ministering to the needy? Talk with your family about practical ways you can serve those less fortunate than you this Christmas.

DAY 11

DEVOTIONAL PASSAGE: LUKE 1:57-66

Take a moment and read Luke 1:57-66. Elizabeth is an older woman, way past her child-birthing years. The birth of her baby is a true miracle. And when we look at verse 58, the reactions of the people back this up. People are excited. They're praising God as a result of this incredible event. But something happens in verse 59 that causes a ripple in the otherwise peaceful narrative.

When Elizabeth goes to name the boy John, just as the angel had instructed her, the people try to put on the brakes. They essentially say, "Hold up. That's not how tradition says that we do this. You don't have anyone in your family named John. Shouldn't you name him after his dad like you're supposed to?" The crazy thing? They didn't even bother to listen to Elizabeth. They go straight to Zechariah. But the cool part is that Zechariah has a little surprise in store.

Read verses 62-66 (remember that Zechariah hasn't been able to talk for months because of his initial doubt that God would bless him with a son). When the people looked to Zechariah to back their play over his wife, he was having no part of it. He supported Elizabeth and God and told the people that their son would be called John. Guess what happened: His obedience was rewarded when God gave him his voice back. This was a sure sign that God was at work. It was just another way that God overturned their understanding of tradition and custom.

We don't always have an awareness of God's plan. It's easy for us to just go with the flow, doing things the way we always have. But if we begin to look for God at work, our expectations get blown wide open. Especially at Christmas, we have to look for God to do huge, God-sized things. And then? We must join Him at His work.

THINK ABOUT THIS:

- Do you try to make God safe and predictable? Do you try to box Him in? If so, why do you think it's our tendency as humans to do this?
- Say a prayer and ask God to help you see through any old customs or traditions keeping you from pursuing Him more.

DEVOTIONAL PASSAGE: ISAIAH 9:6-7, LUKE 1:32-33

Turn to Isaiah 9. Before you read this well-known passage, let's make sure we're good on the context. Isaiah was one of Israel's most important prophets. Isaiah was God's mouthpiece to warn God's people that if they did not turn back to God, they would experience God's judgment. But wrapped up in this pronouncement of coming dread was a hopeful promise of God's faithfulness. That's what we read in verses 6-7. Go ahead and read them now.

If you recall back to when Zechariah encountered the angel in the Temple, you'll remember the angel's announcement echoed God's words in Isaiah 9. Isaiah 9:7 says of the predicted Messiah, "Of the increase of his government and of peace there will be no end, on the throne of David and over his kingdom, to establish it and to uphold it with justice and with righteousness from this time forth and forevermore." When the angel appeared to Zechariah, he said, "And the Lord God will give to him the throne of his father David, and he will reign over the house of Jacob forever, and of his kingdom there will be no end" (Luke 1:32-33). Pretty cool, right? This is a very clear move on God's part to clue in people that Jesus was God's Son, promised centuries before His birth.

When we see prophecies fulfilled, it gives us confidence that God can accomplish His purposes. And so when we see in Isaiah 9 that the coming Messiah will be the Wonderful Counselor, we can trust that Jesus can meet the needs of our hearts. When we read that Jesus is the Mighty God, we can know that the one we serve is Lord over all things. When we read that Jesus is the Prince of Peace, we can trust Him to calm the turmoil in our lives.

Knowing exactly how the birth of Jesus was a part of God's big-picture plan assures us. Which, when it comes to our faith and our lives, is a really big deal.

THINK ABOUT THIS:

- Is there something going on in your life where you need to be assured of God's ability to handle it? If so, now's a good time to think about the truths of who Jesus is.
- Write a prayer to God, asking Him to remind you of who He is. Rest in the truth that He is in control of all things.

DAY 13

DEVOTIONAL PASSAGE: LUKE 1:67-80

This day's devotional will be our final visit with Zechariah and Elizabeth. It's interesting that they play such a prominent role in the Christmas story, isn't it? The reason is that God's plan all along was to have the respective ministries of John and Jesus be linked. John went ahead of Jesus and paved the way for Jesus' message. Their lives were entwined, and so it makes sense that their births would be as well. And so it's fitting that we've given Zechariah and Elizabeth their due.

As we wrap up our look at this couple, read Luke 1:67-80. You've just read Zechariah's response to seeing God keep His promise of giving Zechariah and Elizabeth a son. (Can you imagine what a big day this would have been for Zechariah???) It's in looking closely at Zechariah's response that we understand why it's such a valuable aspect of the Christmas narrative.

What we see Zechariah doing here in verses 68-75 is starting up the ol' time machine and walking us through a little history session. He recalls the promise God made to Abraham to make a nation through him. He recalls God's faithfulness in promising a Messiah to rescue Israel from exile. He sees the promise of Jesus' birth to Mary and Joseph through the lens of God's faithfulness in providing him and Elizabeth with a son. He is grasping the history-altering, world-rocking mission of God. Zechariah is starting to sense that something pretty awesome is happening.

Check out what he says in verses 68-69: "Blessed be the Lord God of Israel, for he has visited and redeemed his people and has raised up a horn of salvation for us in the house of his servant David." Isn't this what Christmas is all about? Isn't this why we get so excited this time of year? Jesus was God wrapped in flesh, hanging out with us, His children. Jesus was God's pathway to peace and harmony between humankind and Himself. And it all started with a little baby born in humble surroundings. This is why we celebrate.

THINK ABOUT THIS:
- In your own words, come up with why Christmas means so much to you.
- What is your favorite thing about Christmas to celebrate?
- Is there anything you can do mentally or spiritually to put yourself in a position to make Christmas more meaningful?

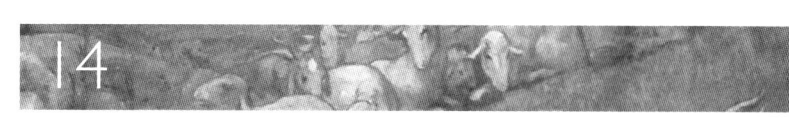

DEVOTIONAL PASSAGE: LUKE 2:1-5

Timing is everything. Timing is the difference between a base hit and an out. Timing is the difference between a well-delivered joke and a lame attempt at humor. Do you slow down for that yellow light or speed up? Timing. Want to go to prom with your crush? Better make sure you don't mess up the timing of your ask. Too late, and you're sitting at home alone.

Here's a truth for you to remember: God's timing is always perfect. Always.

Read Luke 2:1-5. The cool thing about this part of the story has everything to do with God's timing. But to truly understand it, we have to know a little something about the Old Testament Book of Micah. Micah was a prophet preaching God's Word about 750 years before Jesus was born. In Micah 5:2, we read these words: "But you, O Bethlehem Ephrathah, who are too little to be among the clans of Judah, from you shall come forth for me one who is to be ruler in Israel, whose coming forth is from of old, from ancient days." This is a prophecy predicting where the Messiah was to be born. Cool, right? There's only one problem: Jesus, the Messiah, didn't live in Bethlehem. He lived in Nazareth, a roughly 80-mile journey.

So, here's where timing comes in. Caesar Augustus, the Roman Emperor at the time, decided he wanted to count his people. He wanted to see how many people were in his realm for tax purposes. Now, we know that God is in control of all things. Nothing happens without His knowledge or permission. We can rightly say that God used this secular ruler to set in motion His plan. And so it was that Mary and Joseph found themselves in Bethlehem at the exact moment that Jesus would be born. Did I mention that God's timing is perfect?

Christmas is a time of wonder. Take great wonder and awe in the fact there is no one like God. There is no detail too small for His notice. There is no obstacle too big. God orders the universe. He knows the paths of people, time, nature, and events. He brings all things to His purposes. The Christmas story is arguably the crowning achievement of His sovereignty. Let this lead you to praise and worship this season.

THINK ABOUT THIS:

• Look around you. What do you see that points to God's powerful control over all things?
• How can you have an attitude of awe over the last few weeks of this Christmas season? What can you do to make sure you're not missing out on who God is or how He works in your world?

DAY 15

DEVOTIONAL PASSAGE: LUKE 2:6-7

Today you're going to read two verses that describe Jesus' birth. Yes, Christmas is still a week and a half away. Don't worry. You'll revisit them. But it's good to spend some time reading about this event now. Why? For starters, because we can't read it enough, but there's a second reason. The idea of reading this passage now is so that you have the next few days to reflect on it. While we should spend time reflecting on the Gospel all year long, the opportunity for the focused devotion that comes with the Christmas season is a relatively short one. You should spend as much time as possible, reflecting on the birth of Christ.

Read Luke 2:6-7. Slow down and focus on it. See if you can imagine what it must have been like in that stable, which most scholars believe was more likely a cave than a barn. Can you imagine? Animals. Hay. The sights and sounds of giving birth. A newborn baby. An excited father. An exhausted mother. And through it all, there in the manger, the Son of God lies still.

Can you imagine what could be going through Mary and Joseph's minds? What a rush! God had seen them through this challenge. This holy pregnancy that had to have caused drama? It was over. God had done what He said He would do.

Luke 2:7 says that Jesus was Mary's firstborn son. How amazing it is that the eternal Son of God willingly chose to step into our world and take on the power of a "birthday." What does that mean? Think about it. God never had to willingly come in the form of the Son to our earth. Jesus never had to lower Himself to take on the form of the very beings He created. We could have been left in our sin. We certainly deserve it. But through the simple act of the Eternal One embracing the concept of a birthday, a pathway was made to God. Humans no longer had to feel separated from God because of their sin. And all of this came to fruition in a stable on a Bethlehem night.

The King had come. The God-baby was born. And nothing has been the same since.

THINK ABOUT THIS:

- Think for a moment where you have encountered the true Christmas story this Christmas season. Isn't it interesting how hard we have to look to find it in our culture?
- Who in your life needs to know about the life-saving story of Jesus? Say a prayer right now that God will allow you to share this amazing story with them.

DEVOTIONAL PASSAGE: GALATIANS 4:3-5

Ask your parents or grandparents sometimes about what it was like to redeem glass soda bottles when they were younger. You see, when your parents and grandparents were kids, soft drinks were still sold in glass bottles. When you finished a drink, you could bring the bottle back, and you'd redeem it for a dime. (This doesn't seem like a lot, but soft drinks were only fifty cents, so it wasn't a bad deal.) This concept seems completely foreign to us now. But not too long ago, redeeming a bottle was a cool way to get some value out of something that certainly didn't seem to have value anymore.

Before we move on with the rest of the Christmas story, we're going to stop right here and focus on this idea of redemption. After all, yesterday we looked at Jesus' birth for the sole purpose of making sure we reflect on it for the week and a half we have remaining before Christmas. So why not look at one way Paul described Jesus' mission to help us reflect on it even more?

Turn to Galatians 4. Galatians is the Apostle Paul's letter written to the Christians in the Roman province of Galatia. In these verses, Paul speaks to the reason why Jesus came to earth: "to redeem those who were under the law, so that we might receive adoption as sons." The picture of redeeming bottles that we mentioned at the outset of this devotion is an interesting parallel. You see, empty bottles have no intrinsic value. They've been robbed of their purpose. But by redeeming them, the bottler is giving them value. The same is true for us.

You see, sin robbed us of our purpose too. Humankind's original sin destroyed the relationship between God and people. We were left broken and used up. Until Jesus redeemed us. By going to the cross in our place, Jesus placed a value on us. He said, in essence, "Your life is worth my life. I will give my life to redeem you." This is why Jesus came. This is what He accomplished.

What ended on the cross started in a manger. A miraculous birth made an atoning death possible.

THINK ABOUT THIS:

• How does the fact that Jesus has redeemed us of our sins empower you to live a life of purpose on this earth?
• We all get down from time to time. How can the truth that Jesus died to redeem your life help lift your spirits when things get tough?

DAY 17

DEVOTIONAL PASSAGE: LUKE 2:8-14

Who are the popular kids in your school? Who are troublemakers? Who are the jocks? Who are the nerds? The problem with these questions isn't necessarily that it's a terrible way to label people. No, the biggest problem is that you could answer them. This doesn't necessarily say anything negative about you. But it does speak to the fact that your school is most likely a place where people are labeled and sorted. Cool kids over here. Weird kids over there. It may just be how it is (it's kind of always been that way), but it doesn't make it right. And it definitely doesn't mean that God is OK with it.

Read Luke 2:8-14. The shepherds are one of the coolest parts of the Christmas narrative. It's so fitting that God would choose them to be the first recipients of the news of His Son's birth. The choosing of the shepherds gives us a glimpse into God's heart.

Shepherds were at the very bottom of the Jewish social ladder. They were thought to be unclean. They weren't welcomed in proper circles. They were outcasts. And so God chose them to be the first people to hear a birth announcement thousands in years in the making. Of course He did. This shouldn't surprise us. God's Kingdom places a tremendous value on those the world says are valueless.

Jesus said, "Blessed are the meek." He said, "The last will be first." He said, "Bring the little ones to me." He said, "The things you did for the least of these? You might as well have been doing for me."

This Christmas season is a wonderful opportunity to align your heart with God's. Become an agent of love and compassion for those the world has passed by. And do so in the name of Christ.

THINK ABOUT THIS:

- It's tough to take a stand in school. It is. But what if you were bold enough to break down the walls created by how we label people? What if you showed kindness to those who need it most, regardless of what "group" they are in? What kind of ripple do you think that would cause in your school?
- What's one thing you and your family can do this Christmas to show God's love to the needy in your community?

DAY 18

DEVOTIONAL PASSAGE: LUKE 2:15-20

Let's focus on the shepherds one more day. They have a lot to teach us about being a Christ-follower. Yesterday we looked at God's birth announcement to the shepherds. Today, let's focus on their response.

Read Luke 2:15-20. The shepherds saw something they weren't expecting. They had an encounter with God's Kingdom in an amazing way. And afterward, they were left with a choice. What were they to do with the information they just heard? The truth is that once we encounter Christ, each of us, you included, has a choice to make.

When people hear the Gospel or have a chance to encounter Christ through the Bible, there is a choice to be made. People have to respond one way or another. They will either move on this information, or they will not. They will either be compelled to know more, or they will choose to walk away.

The shepherds had a choice. They made their choice, and they made it well. The shepherds acted, and they retold. They acted on the angels' message. Look in verse 15. They heard, and they moved. They could have sat and talked, or they could have gone home. But they didn't. They followed through, and they were rewarded by coming face-to-face with the Son of God.

But they didn't stop with simply acting. They retold. Verse 17 says that once they were sure of the angels' message, they couldn't contain themselves. They started talking. They started spreading the word about Jesus. It was as if they couldn't keep quiet.

Today, over two thousand years later, we're still expected to do the same. If you know Christ, you should find yourself compelled to speak of His story. If you have encountered God and His Kingdom, you know that you will find it hard to keep your mouth shut.

You have to move. You have to act. And with God empowering you, you will. And you'll be awesome.

THINK ABOUT THIS:

- What's keeping you from being a more powerful teller of Jesus' story?
- What can you do to be more committed to being someone who tells Jesus' story to others, especially during a time of year ripe for talking about God's message of love and salvation?

DAY  19

DEVOTIONAL PASSAGE: LUKE 2:6-7, REVELATION 19:11-16

As we near the last week before Christmas, let's connect the Christmas narrative with a description of Jesus we see somewhere else in the Bible. Let's look forward in time from the manger and the shepherds and Bethlehem. WAY forward in time. Let's look to the end of the story (which in itself is a beginning).

Read Luke 2:6-7. See Jesus, the God-baby, in the manger. Innocent. Vulnerable as all babies are. Fully God, but 100% human. Fragile. Helpless. Have you got that vision in your mind? Now turn to Revelation 19 and read verses 11-16.

This is the part of John's vision where Jesus engages in the last battle with the forces of evil. Spoiler alert: Jesus wins. The baby born in a manger? He is Faithful and True. He declares war on evil, and even His warring is righteous. The Jesus we see here is on the very edge of being indescribable. John did his God-inspired best, but his human words can barely explain what he saw. This is the full power of Jesus unmasked.

Jesus is the victor. He is the Only King, the Only Lord. Jesus is the warrior who will lead the armies of God against the forces of evil in the end times. He is the sword-bearer who strikes down nations. This is the Jesus bringing victory over evil because evil must be defeated.

There's a week before Christmas. It's super easy to forget who it is we're awaiting. Not only can we lose focus with all the crazy busy-ness that's going on around us, but we can also lose sight of who Jesus truly is. This Jesus? The Jesus on the white horse? It's the very same Jesus that Mary carried in her womb. How can it be? It can only be because, in His great, indescribable love, Jesus came to us, leaving the things of heaven to share in the story with His earth-bound children. And He is worthy of our praise and adoration.

THINK ABOUT THIS:

• Contemplation isn't something we often do in our culture. But thinking deeply about God is one of the best things we can do. Read back through that description of Jesus in Revelation 19. Slowly. Contemplate what you're reading. Let your mind and heart soak in what you read. Isn't Jesus amazing!?

DAY 20

DEVOTIONAL PASSAGE: MATTHEW 2:1-2

Read Matthew 2:1-2. These guys lived in a very different culture than the one we find ourselves in. But despite this fact, we can learn a lot from their example. Especially as we consider the information-rich society we currently live in, where "facts" and "faith" are so often pitted against one another.

We think these men came from somewhere in what was formerly the Babylonian Empire. If this is true, they probably gathered their knowledge of God from the Jewish people's exile in Babylon. The wise man were students of astrology as well as other mystical teachings from multiple cultures. And they also possessed knowledge of world religions, such as their knowledge of God. They would have had a knowledge of the Hebrew God among their knowledge of many other culture's gods. This is the backdrop upon which the wise man processed the sign they saw in the sky.

When the wise men saw an unusual stellar occurrence, recorded in verse 2, they recognized it for what it was: the hand of someone mighty. If it's true that these mystics had a knowledge of God, then it's possible they knew the Old Testament prophecies relating to the coming of a Messiah. But knowing and acting are two different things. And that is what we can learn from these wise men.

These mystics saw the evidence and acted upon it. Their faith may or may not have turned into a saving faith in God. However, they expressed a faith that wasn't frustrated by their intellectuality. Quite the opposite. Their knowledge fueled their faith. Their deep understanding compelled them to act. Theirs was a seeking faith!

For so many in our culture, and maybe for you, our perceived "knowledge" can sometimes be a barrier to our faith. The wise men serve as a wonderful example that this never has to be the case.

THINK ABOUT THIS:

- Why do you think our culture makes such a strong distinction between "fact" and "faith"? Do you believe the two are incompatible? Or do you think there is room for harmony between the two?
- How do you deal with your questions and doubts? Have you ever been uneasy about owning them? What keeps you from taking your questions to God and seeking an answer?

DAY

DEVOTIONAL PASSAGE: MATTHEW 2:3-6

Life throws the proverbial "curve balls" at us, right? Stuff we don't expect. Things we can't predict. It's the same for everyone. Often what makes us unique is how we respond to the unexpected. When an opportunity presents itself, the difference is whether you respond by seizing it or letting it pass you by. Our response is everything.

Read Matthew 2:3-6. We introduced the wise men yesterday. We discussed how the wise men responded to what they saw. If we were to describe the wise men's response, we might use words like "curious" or "questioning," or maybe even "seeking." However you describe it, the point is that the wise men saw something in the stars they regularly studied, and rightly interpreted it as a sign that something spectacular happened. Their response was the right one: they sought out Jesus, the King of the Jews.

Let's stop for a moment and study Herod's response. Herod was the Roman-appointed governor over the region. He was a pretty brutal leader. And instead of being curious about the spiritual implications of Jesus' birth, his response was different. Herod was calculating, paranoid, and power-hungry. He was scared that Jesus would somehow diminish his status. He was fearful of who this newborn King might be.

In the wise men and Herod, we see the same responses people still have to Jesus today. People either hear about Jesus and are curious about who He is and what He can do in and through them, or they are dismissive, fearful, or downright apathetic.

Your life is like an advertisement for Jesus. The way you live tells the world that you belong to Christ. People will respond to Jesus in you. And their response will either be curious or dismissive. Your role is to be faithful in communicating Christ, especially this Christmas season

THINK ABOUT THIS:
- How do you share God's message of hope and salvation with the world around you? What are some examples of what this looks like?
- What is one very practical, Christmas-centered way you can share the Gospel with others in the next few days?

DAY  22

DEVOTIONAL PASSAGE: MATTHEW 2:9-12

This will be the last day that we spend looking at the wise men. And their story has one more thing to teach us about. Their story can teach us a very powerful lesson on worship.

Read Matthew 2:9-12. The wise men leave Herod, and God uses a star to lead them to the manger, where they encounter Jesus. Look at verse 11. How did they respond? They responded in worship. And in their response, we see a really simple definition of worship. Worship is what happens when we see God, and we know we've seen God, and then respond accordingly. It can look different ways. But worship is always the response to an authentic encounter with God.

Our desire to worship God goes way beyond what we do in church on Sunday mornings. After all, your life intersects with God in many different ways. You encounter Him in His Word. You may think about Him on your way to school, listening to praise music in the car. You experience or are aware of the ways God has blessed you. You see God in His creation, and so on. These are all encounters with God. And when you encounter God in these ways, when you behold Him, worship is your response.

Here's the cool thing: anytime we encounter God, we can worship Him. And so you can and should worship God in the car, alone. You can worship God in how you treat people. You can worship God through corporate praise in your church community. You can worship God with friends over ice cream.

A lifestyle of worship is the way a Gospel-centered Christ-follower shows God his or her gratitude. Worship is simply giving back to God what is rightfully His.

You've certainly encountered God a lot over the last few weeks. (That's one of the best parts about Christmas.) Have you spent enough time responding to Him in worship?

THINK ABOUT THIS:

- Worship is something we are to do with our lives each day. Can you think of some ways you might worship God as you go throughout your everyday life?
- What if you were to have a family worship time tonight before you go to bed? What would it look like? Are you brave enough to get one organized?

DEVOTIONAL PASSAGE: MALACHI 4:1-6

Christmas is two days away. Tomorrow is Christmas Eve. The hope is that you have used the last several weeks to prepare your heart and mind so that you are in the right frame of mind to experience Christmas. In a word, the hope is that you are properly "expectant."

What does it mean to be expectant? To be expectant means to be in a state of expecting. When we expect something, we're looking for it—waiting on it. There is a certain longing in our spirits for the thing we're waiting on. And if you've used the last few weeks accordingly, you should be properly expecting Jesus.

Do you know who else was expecting Jesus? The Israelites. His chosen people. For a few hundred years, many of the people had actively rebelled against God. They had turned from Him and worshipped other gods. God spoke through His prophets to try and turn the people back, being super patient with them as they were unfaithful to Him. And then, He could be patient no more. He allowed the judgment He predicted to come true. Israel was destroyed. The people were left isolated and desolated. And the faithful among them longed for God. They were waiting expectantly.

Read Malachi 4:1-6. These are the very last words of the Old Testament. Scholars believe there was roughly a 400-year period between these words and the words of the New Testament. And during this entire period, the people were waiting. Waiting. Waiting.

Look at Malachi's words here: "Behold the day is coming." Malachi was longing for God to return and judge the evildoers in his land. This would be a bad day for those who were against God. But for the righteous, the day will come like the dawning of the sun, shining new light on all the people of God. Malachi didn't quite know what to expect. He didn't quite know what he was waiting for. But he knew he was waiting on God's promise to come true.

Jesus was what Malachi was waiting on. Jesus was the object of the people's expectations. The question for you, as you near Christmas Eve, is whether Jesus is the object of YOUR expectation.

THINK ABOUT THIS:

- If you've put yourself in the position to properly expect God this Christmas season, how has this impacted your faith?
- If you haven't, no worries. What can you do to get yourself ready to take in everything that Christmas means?

CHRISTMAS DAY // DEVOTIONAL PASSAGE: ZECHARIAH 9:9

Rejoice! The King is coming.

Tonight, our hearts are joy-filled as we celebrate the coming of the King. But this King doesn't come as other kings before Him. He does not ride in on war-horse, his vast armies going before him. He does not come on the stairs of the government, overthrowing his enemies. He does not come in brash arrogance and inflated self-pride as those before and after him.

This King comes quietly.

Though He is the most powerful of all, He comes meekly.

Though His Kingdom reign is absolute, He asks of those who would join His realm only that they would come.

Though He alone holds the power to turn back the tide of death itself, He comes as a human baby, frail and fragile.

Though He is the One who hung the stars in place and stretched out the boundaries for the sea, He willingly, lovingly chooses to wrap Himself in humanity to save the very beings He created.

And so celebrate tonight, in thankfulness, in humility, as those who have been pulled from the grave and given life, all through the work of the King that began in the most humbling of surroundings. Celebrate the Christ-child.

He is born. Rejoice.

"REJOICE GREATLY, O DAUGHTER OF ZION! SHOUT ALOUD, O DAUGHTER OF JERUSALEM! BEHOLD, YOUR KING IS COMING TO YOU; RIGHTEOUS AND HAVING SALVATION IS HE, HUMBLE AND MOUNTED ON A DONKEY, ON A COLT, THE FOAL OF A DONKEY." –ZECHARIAH 9:9

DAY 24

CHRISTMAS EVE (FAMILY DEVOTIONAL)

For this family devotional, have your family gather together with a Bible. If you want to arrange to have a candle in the middle of where you're gathered, even better. Light the candle and turn off the lights.

FIRST, choose a parent to read the birth narrative from Luke 2:1-20.

THEN, take turns going around the room, sharing reflections. Consider having someone ask questions similar to the following:
- What feelings or emotions does this story generate in you?
- What is your favorite part of the story?
- In your own words, why is this such an important moment in history?
- What do you think Mary or Joseph or the shepherds must have been thinking?

FINALLY, spend some time in prayer going around the room and thanking God for sending His Son to make way for us to be in relationship with Him.

Consider closing by singing a hymn together, such as "Silent Night," or another favorite that celebrates Christ's birth.

DAY 25

CHRISTMAS DAY // DEVOTIONAL PASSAGE: COLOSSIANS 1:15-20

As you focus on Christ this day, take in the glory of these two passages, one that speaks to His birth, and one that speaks of He whose birth we celebrate. They are one and the same.

[6] And while they were there, the time came for her to give birth. [7] And she gave birth to her first-born son and wrapped him in swaddling cloths and laid him in a manger, because there was no place for them in the inn.
⊠ Luke 2:6-7

[15] He is the image of the invisible God, the firstborn of all creation. [16] For by him all things were created, in heaven and on earth, visible and invisible, whether thrones or dominions or rulers or author-ities—all things were created through him and for him. [17] And he is before all things, and in him all things hold together. [18] And he is the head of the body, the church. He is the beginning, the firstborn from the dead, that in everything he might be preeminent. [19] For in him all the fullness of God was pleased to dwell, [20] and through him to reconcile to himself all things, whether on earth or in heaven, making peace by the blood of his cross. ⊠ Colossians 1:15-20

This is the baby that was born. This is He whom we celebrate.

Merry Christmas.

DAY 25

CHRISTMAS EVE (FAMILY DEVOTIONAL)

Merry Christmas!

For your family devotional, we're going to keep it simple.

FIRST, take a moment and re-read the verses aloud from your Christmas Day devotional on page 29.

THEN, take turns going around and saying one specific thing you are thankful for this Christmas.

FINALLY, have someone say a prayer of praise to God for His great love for us.

ANDY BLANKS

Andy Blanks is the Publisher and Co-Founder of YM360 and Iron Hill Press. A former Marine, he has worked in youth ministry, mostly in the field of publishing, for nearly 20 years. During that time, Andy has led the development of some of the most popular Bible study curriculum and discipleship resources in the country. He has authored numerous books, Bible studies, and articles, and regularly speaks at events and conferences, both for adults and teenagers. But Andy's passion is communicating the transforming truth of the Bible, which he does in his local church on a weekly basis.

Andy and his wife, Brendt, were married in 2000. They have four children, three girls and one boy.

YOU KNOW IT'S IMPORTANT TO GROW CLOSER TO GOD

YM360 DEVOTIONALS CAN HELP

Student devotionals from YM360 help you stay close to God by equipping you to creatively and relevantly dig-in to His Word.

CHECK OUT THE AWESOME SELECTION OF DEVOTIONAL BOOKS AT YM360.COM